fo

D0831779

SACRED SPACE

from the website www.sacredspace.ie
Prayer from the Irish Jesuits

LOYOLA PRESS.
A JESUIT MINISTRY
Chicago

LOYOLA PRESS.
A JESUIT MINISTRY
www.loyolapress.com

This edition of *Sacred Space for Lent* is published by arrangement
with Messenger Publications, 37 Lower Leeson Street, Dublin D02
W938, Ireland.

Scripture quotations are from *New Revised Standard Version Bible:
Anglicised Catholic Edition*, copyright © 1989, 1993 National
Council of the Churches of Christ in the United States of America.
Used by permission. All rights reserved.

Loyola Press in Chicago thanks the Irish Jesuits and Messenger
Press for preparing this book for publication.

Cover art credit: Kathryn Seckman Kirsch

ISBN-13: 978-0-8294-5581-6

Printed in the United States of America.
23 24 25 26 27 Versa 10 9 8 7 6 5 4 3 2 1

Contents

Sacred Space Prayer

Bless all who worship you, almighty God,
from the rising of the sun to its setting;
from your goodness enrich us,
by your love inspire us,
by your Spirit guide us,
by your power protect us,
in your mercy receive us,
now and always.

How to Use This Booklet

During each week of Lent, begin by reading the 'Something to think and pray about each day this week'. Then go through the 'Presence of God', 'Freedom' and 'Consciousness' steps to help you prepare yourself to hear the Word of God speaking to you. In the next step, 'The Word', turn to the Scripture reading for each day of the week. Inspiration points are provided if you need them. Then return to the 'Conversation' and 'Conclusion' steps. Follow this process every day of Lent.

14–17 February 2024

Something to think and pray about each day this week:

Archbishop Joe Cassidy, late of Tuam, often said that 'Prayer is the oxygen of our faith.' The language of the liturgy becomes a foundation to help our ongoing spiritual development as well as conversion, because faith-beliefs anchor as well as guide us in the way we live.

The short Latin prepositions of the Eucharistic doxology—'*per*', '*cum*', '*in*'—give us a significant script for our daily lives as Christians: through Christ, with Christ and in Christ. Whatever we do or say, wherever we live, we do all through, with and in Christ. After all, he is Emmanuel, God-with-us.

Pope Francis has offered us a celebrated maxim that the Eucharist, 'although it is the fullness of sacramental life, is not a prize for the perfect, but a powerful medicine and nourishment for the weak'. The people of God include all those who accept Jesus' invitation to sit at the table of communion and community to celebrate his real presence at the 'supper of the Lamb'.

As we pray this doxology at Mass or silently in the depths of our hearts in our quieter moments, may it be the core of our beliefs about ourselves and all our relationships.

John Cullen, *The Sacred Heart Messenger*,
September 2022

The Presence of God

'Come to me, all you who are weary and are carrying heavy burdens, and I will give you rest.' Here I am, Lord. I come to seek your presence. I long for your healing power.

Freedom

God is not foreign to my freedom. The Spirit breathes life into my most intimate desires, gently nudging me towards all that is good. I ask for the grace to let myself be enfolded by the Spirit.

Consciousness

I remind myself that I am in the presence of the Lord. I will take refuge in his loving heart. He is my strength in times of weakness. He is my comforter in times of sorrow.

The Word

I take my time to read the word of God slowly, a few times, allowing myself to dwell on anything that strikes me. *(Please turn to the Scripture on the following pages. Inspiration points are there, should you need them. When you are ready, return here to continue.)*

Conversation

Jesus, you always welcomed little children when you walked on this earth. Teach me to have a childlike trust in you. Teach me to live in the knowledge that you will never abandon me.

Conclusion

Glory be to the Father, and to the Son, and to the Holy Spirit, as it was in the beginning, is now and ever shall be, world without end. Amen.

Wednesday 14 February
Ash Wednesday
Matthew 6:1–6, 16–18

'Beware of practising your piety before others in order to be seen by them; for then you have no reward from your Father in heaven.

'So whenever you give alms, do not sound a trumpet before you, as the hypocrites do in the synagogues and in the streets, so that they may be praised by others. Truly I tell you, they have received their reward. But when you give alms, do not let your left hand know what your right hand is doing, so that your alms may be done in secret; and your Father who sees in secret will reward you.

'And whenever you pray, do not be like the hypocrites; for they love to stand and pray in the synagogues and at the street corners, so that they may be seen by others. Truly I tell you, they have received their reward. But whenever you pray, go into your room and shut the door and pray to your Father who is in secret; and your Father who sees in secret will reward you.

'And whenever you fast, do not look dismal, like the hypocrites, for they disfigure their faces so as to show others that they are fasting. Truly I tell you, they have received their reward. But when you fast, put oil on your head and wash your face, so that your fasting may be seen not by others but by your Father who is in secret; and your Father who sees in secret will reward you.'

- The invitation in Lent is to turn towards God in true worship. Attention is drawn to some possible pitfalls, to areas where we can be too centred on ourselves and our own glory. We pray for the freedom to turn to the Lord for direction that will keep us focused, as we need guidance to travel the road that the Lord has taken.

- Almsgiving, prayer and fasting are significant aspects of our lives and of our relationship with the Lord and others. We are called to give glory to God, bringing us beyond selfish interests that can dominate. Lord, we desire to walk with you, but we need your help to do so, strengthened by your example and teaching.

Thursday 15 February
Luke 9:22–25

Jesus said to them, 'The Son of Man must undergo great suffering, and be rejected by the elders, chief priests, and scribes, and be killed, and on the third day be raised.'

Then he said to them all, 'If any want to become my followers, let them deny themselves and take up their cross daily and follow me. For those who want to save their life will lose it, and those who lose their life for my sake will save it. What does it profit them if they gain the whole world, but lose or forfeit themselves?'

- We have begun our journey towards Jerusalem with Jesus and we are reminded about what it entails. Jesus' teaching and way of life would challenge the existing system and be too much for the religious leaders. Lord, we tend to shy away from suffering—give us the strength and courage to stay with you, knowing that your death is the way to life.

- Jesus reminds us that his call involves self-denial and forgoing our own way. We follow his way and are asked to respond as he did. Being asked to take up one's cross means living like Jesus and for him. Lord, show us what is of lasting value and where true profit is to be found.

Friday 16 February
Matthew 9:14–15

Then the disciples of John came to him, saying, 'Why do we and the Pharisees fast often, but your disciples do not fast?' And Jesus said to them, 'The wedding-guests cannot mourn as long as the bridegroom is with them, can they? The days will come when the bridegroom is taken away from them, and then they will fast.'

- John the Baptist's life was ascetic. He lived in the wilderness and ate locusts and wild honey, advocating a similar life-style for his followers. It was very different from the reports they were hearing about Jesus attending dinners. This Lent, help us fast from all that is divisive and critical in our relationships with others.

- Jesus reminded his hearers that he would not be with them always from an earthly perspective. They were to be glad and to celebrate while he was with them in a physical and personal way. Lord, you are the bridegroom, our friend, who invites us to rejoice with you. Give us the strength to continue to do what is right at all times.

Saturday 17 February
Luke 5:27–32

After this he went out and saw a tax-collector named Levi, sitting at the tax booth; and he said to him, 'Follow me.' And he got up, left everything, and followed him.

Then Levi gave a great banquet for him in his house; and there was a large crowd of tax-collectors and others sitting at the table with them. The Pharisees and their scribes were complaining to his disciples, saying, 'Why do you eat and drink with tax-collectors and sinners?' Jesus answered, 'Those who are well have no need of a physician, but those who are sick; I have come to call not the righteous but sinners to repentance.'

- Jesus called Levi, a tax collector, as a disciple. Caravaggio depicts Levi caught in a dilemma, with one hand pointing to himself as if to say, 'You are calling me?', his other hand on the money he had collected. Lord, we also are unlikely choices but you call us. Help us to let go of what we cling to so readily so that we are freer to follow you.

- A range of people interacted with Jesus, who reached out to all. To let Jesus lead seemed to be too much for the Pharisees, who were critical of his teaching and his actions in befriending tax collectors and sinners. Give us what we need to hear your call afresh and to respond with generosity.

The First Week of Lent
18–24 February 2024

Something to think and pray about each day this week:

Too often we think of Lent as a time to give things up, rather than time to take on something new. Ask yourself how you can respond to Christ's call in a more proactive way this Lent. To do so it might be good to make a regular examination of conscience, something St Ignatius encouraged. Think about:

1. The gifts I have received from God during the day that I can be thankful for.
2. Where I have cooperated with God during the day. Where I have not worked with God but given in to sinful elements within me, neglecting what God wants of me.
3. The forgiveness God offers me for the times when I have not responded to his presence and love in my life.
4. How God's help will guide me through things to come and how the Holy Spirit will be with me.

Do this examination of conscience daily during Lent and see how it draws you closer to an awareness of God's presence in your life and of the kind of life God is calling you to lead.

Pat Corkery, *The Sacred Heart Messenger*,
March 2022

The Presence of God

What is present to me is what has a hold on my becoming. I reflect on the presence of God always there in love, amidst the many things that have a hold on me. I pause and pray that I may let God affect my becoming in this precise moment.

Freedom

By God's grace I was born to live in freedom. Free to enjoy the pleasures he created for me. Dear Lord, grant that I may live as you intended, with complete confidence in your loving care.

Consciousness

I exist in a web of relationships: links to nature, people, God. I trace out these links, giving thanks for the life that flows through them. Some links are twisted or broken; I may feel regret, anger, disappointment. I pray for the gift of acceptance and forgiveness.

The Word

God speaks to each of us individually. I listen attentively to hear what he is saying to me. Read the text a few times, then listen. *(Please turn to the Scripture on the following pages. Inspiration points are there, should you need them. When you are ready, return here to continue.)*

Conversation

I begin to talk with Jesus about the Scripture I have just read. What part of it strikes a chord in me? Perhaps the words of a friend—or some story I have heard recently—will rise to the surface in my consciousness. If so, does the story throw light on what the Scripture passage may be saying to me?

Conclusion

Glory be to the Father, and to the Son, and to the Holy Spirit, as it was in the beginning, is now and ever shall be, world without end. Amen.

Sunday 18 February
First Sunday of Lent
Mark 1:12–15

And the Spirit immediately drove him out into the wilderness. He was in the wilderness for forty days, tempted by Satan; and he was with the wild beasts; and the angels waited on him.

Now after John was arrested, Jesus came to Galilee, proclaiming the good news of God, and saying, 'The time is fulfilled, and the kingdom of God has come near; repent, and believe in the good news.'

- Immediately after Jesus' baptism and the affirmation of his mission 'the Spirit immediately drove him out into the wilderness.' It was seen as a place of testing, but it was also where God could be found. Lord, give us the Spirit to help us to recognise the challenging aspects of living out our baptism, so that we are not complacent.

Monday 19 February
Matthew 25:31–46

'When the Son of Man comes in his glory, and all the angels with him, then he will sit on the throne of his glory. All the nations will be gathered before him, and he will separate people one from another as a shepherd separates the sheep from the goats, and he will put the sheep at his right hand and the goats at the left.

Then the king will say to those at his right hand, "Come, you that are blessed by my Father, inherit the kingdom prepared for you from the foundation of the world; for I was hungry and you gave me food, I was thirsty and you gave me something to drink, I was a stranger and you welcomed me, I was naked and you gave me clothing, I was sick and you took care of me, I was in prison and you visited me." Then the righteous will answer him, "Lord, when was it that we saw you hungry and gave you food, or thirsty and gave you something to drink? And when was it that we saw you a stranger and welcomed you, or naked and gave you clothing? And when was it that we saw you sick or in prison and visited you?" And the king will answer them, "Truly I tell you, just as you did it to one of the least of these who are members of my family, you did it to me." Then he will say to those at his left hand, "You that are accursed, depart from me into the eternal fire prepared for the devil and his angels; for I was hungry and you gave me no food, I was thirsty and you gave me nothing to drink, I was a stranger and you did not welcome me, naked and you did not give me clothing, sick and in prison and you did not visit me." Then they also will answer, "Lord, when was it that we saw you hungry or thirsty or a stranger or naked or sick or in prison, and did not take care of you?" Then he will answer them, "Truly I tell you, just as you did not do it to one of the least of these, you did not do it to me." And these will go away into eternal punishment, but the righteous into eternal life.'

- The qualities desired are those of the 'corporal works of mercy', which deal with genuine concern for those on the margins of life. Jesus cared for the most vulnerable and reminds us that we are to do the same. Lord, give us the freedom to move beyond our comfort zones to reach out to those in need, for you are present in them.

- The reading speaks about more than passing actions as it calls for converted hearts. Ultimately, we will be judged on love, or perhaps we will judge ourselves on how we respond to those in need. Lord, give us compassionate hearts and heal us of the prejudices that can blind us to their presence in life.

Tuesday 20 February

Matthew 6:7–15

'When you are praying, do not heap up empty phrases as the Gentiles do; for they think that they will be heard because of their many words. Do not be like them, for your Father knows what you need before you ask him.

'Pray then in this way:
Our Father in heaven,
  hallowed be your name.
  Your kingdom come.
  Your will be done,
  on earth as it is in heaven.
  Give us this day our daily bread.
  And forgive us our debts,
  as we also have forgiven our debtors.
  And do not bring us to the time of trial,
  but rescue us from the evil one.

For if you forgive others their trespasses, your heavenly Father will also forgive you; but if you do not forgive others, neither will your Father forgive your trespasses.'

- We pray 'Our Father', not 'my Father'. We are on a journey together. Forgiveness is central to good relationships. We pray to the Lord for his forgiveness, to be able to forgive ourselves and each other, knowing that the Lord is bigger than our failures.

Wednesday 21 February
Luke 11:29–32

When the crowds were increasing, he began to say, 'This generation is an evil generation; it asks for a sign, but no sign will be given to it except the sign of Jonah. For just as Jonah became a sign to the people of Nineveh, so the Son of Man will be to this generation.

The queen of the South will rise at the judgement with the people of this generation and condemn them, because she came from the ends of the earth to listen to the wisdom of Solomon, and see, something greater than Solomon is here! The people of Nineveh will rise up at the judgement with this generation and condemn it, because they repented at the proclamation of Jonah, and see, something greater than Jonah is here!'

- Jonah was the reluctant prophet to the Ninevites. When he did go and proclaim the message, the people repented and changed their evil ways. Jesus drew on the story of Jonah to teach. Lord, touch our hearts that we may be converted to you and your message.

- Prophets proclaimed the truth of God's message and prepared the way for Jesus. They announced the good news that was to be fulfilled in Jesus, who was greater than the prophets, being the Son of God, the Word incarnate. We ask that we may come to deeper repentance so that we might strengthen our relationship with Jesus.

Thursday 22 February
The Chair of St Peter
Matthew 16:13–19

Now when Jesus came into the district of Caesarea Philippi, he asked his disciples, 'Who do people say that the Son of Man is?' And they said, 'Some say John the Baptist, but others Elijah, and still others Jeremiah or one of the prophets.' He said to them, 'But who do you say that I am?' Simon Peter answered, 'You are the Messiah, the Son of the living God.' And Jesus answered him, 'Blessed are you, Simon son of Jonah! For flesh and blood has not revealed this to you, but my Father in heaven. And I tell you, you are Peter, and on this rock I will build my church, and the gates of Hades will not prevail against it. I will give you the keys of the kingdom of heaven, and whatever you bind on earth will be bound in heaven, and whatever you loose on earth will be loosed in heaven.'

- This is not about a chair, but about its occupant, who is a source of unity among believers. Authority is meant to be for service. May our relationship with Jesus be a source of strength to us so that we can grow more fully into the unity he desires.

- This gospel is not simply information about Jesus, but is about a prophetic call to a personal relationship. Lord, you reassure us of your support. May we live it out in a personal and prophetic way.

Friday 23 February
Matthew 5:20–26

Jesus said to them, 'For I tell you, unless your righteousness exceeds that of the scribes and Pharisees, you will never enter the kingdom of heaven.

'You have heard that it was said to those of ancient times, "You shall not murder"; and "whoever murders shall be liable to judgement." But I say to you that if you are angry with a brother or sister, you will be liable to judgement; and if you insult a brother or sister, you will be liable to the council; and if you say, "You fool", you will be liable to the hell of fire. So when you are offering your gift at the altar, if you remember that your brother or sister has something against you, leave your gift there before the altar and go; first be reconciled to your brother or sister, and then come and offer your gift. Come to terms quickly with your accuser while you are on the way to court with him, or your accuser may hand you over to the judge, and the judge to the guard, and you will be thrown into prison. Truly I tell you, you will never get out until you have paid the last penny.'

- Jesus' kingdom was in marked contrast to the kingdoms of the world. The scribes and Pharisees were trapped by externals and by their role in society. We pray to recognise where external factors have too much importance for us, so that we can choose to look to the Lord and his kingdom of justice, love and peace.

Saturday 24 February
Matthew 5:43–48

Jesus said, 'You have heard that it was said, "You shall love your neighbour and hate your enemy." But I say to you, Love your enemies and pray for those who persecute you, so that you may be children of your Father in heaven; for he makes his sun rise on the evil and on the good, and sends rain on the righteous and on the unrighteous. For if you love those who love you, what reward do you have? Do not even the tax-collectors do the same? And if you greet only your brothers and sisters, what more are you doing than others? Do not even the Gentiles do the same? Be perfect, therefore, as your heavenly Father is perfect.'

- God loves all that God has made (Wisdom 11:24), and all that God has created is good (Genesis 1:12, 25, 31). That provides a lens through which to look at life and relationships. Human factors, such as jealousy and envy, can get in the way of the harmony God desires. May we have a vision that is inclusive, open to all.

- There is a clear tendency in our time to label people and make that label stick for ever. One failure can be allowed to categorise someone for life. Living by selfish human categories does not respect the inherent dignity of each person. Lord, we pray to see beyond the externals to the dignity of each person as loved into existence by you.

The Second Week of Lent
25 February–2 March 2024

Something to think and pray about each day this week:

Jesus heard at the Transfiguration that he was beloved! We all want to know that someone would say that they love us.

We are God's favoured ones. We live in the big, wide world of God's love, and Jesus on Tabor was allowing himself to be loved in the radiant light of God, shining even in the cloud.

Together we are loved as Peter, James and John were loved in community. Light is caught from one to the other. We are the light of Tabor Mountain for each other—all are loved. Those whom I like and those I like less! The radiant body of Christ was hammered and killed later by ourselves. Love killed at Calvary rose again. Love cannot die.

We can transfigure or disfigure each other. We can bring out the light and the hope and the joy in our belonging to God!

We can transfigure a school, a parish, a community or any group by first of all our being loved by God and letting love emit from ourselves. If we really believe we are loved by God, then the world we live in is transfigured—changed utterly.

Donal Neary SJ,
*Gospel Reflections for
Sundays of Year B*

The Presence of God

'Be still, and know that I am God!' Lord, your words lead us to the calmness and greatness of your presence.

Freedom

'In these days, God taught me as a schoolteacher teaches a pupil' (St Ignatius). I remind myself that there are things God has to teach me yet, and I ask for the grace to hear them and let them change me.

Consciousness

How am I really feeling? Lighthearted? Heavyhearted? I may be very much at peace, happy to be here. Equally, I may be frustrated, worried or angry. I acknowledge how I really am. It is the real me whom the Lord loves.

The Word

God speaks to each of us individually. I listen attentively to hear what he is saying to me. Read the text a few times, then listen. *(Please turn to the Scripture on the following pages. Inspiration points are there, should you need them. When you are ready, return here to continue.)*

Conversation

Do I notice myself reacting as I pray with the word of God? Do I feel challenged, comforted, angry?

Imagining Jesus sitting or standing by me, I speak out my feelings, as one trusted friend to another.

Conclusion

I thank God for these moments we have spent together and for any insights I have been given concerning the text.

Sunday 25 February
Second Sunday of Lent

Mark 9:2–10

Six days later, Jesus took with him Peter and James and John, and led them up a high mountain apart, by themselves. And he was transfigured before them, and his clothes became dazzling white, such as no one on earth could bleach them. And there appeared to them Elijah with Moses, who were talking with Jesus. Then Peter said to Jesus, 'Rabbi, it is good for us to be here; let us make three dwellings, one for you, one for Moses, and one for Elijah.' He did not know what to say, for they were terrified. Then a cloud overshadowed them, and from the cloud there came a voice, 'This is my Son, the Beloved; listen to him!' Suddenly when they looked around, they saw no one with them any more, but only Jesus.

As they were coming down the mountain, he ordered them to tell no one about what they had seen, until after the Son of Man had risen from the dead. So they kept the matter to themselves, questioning what this rising from the dead could mean.

- The Transfiguration, which reveals something further of Jesus' identity, comes immediately after the first prediction of his Passion. Jesus was fulfilling both the Law and the prophets, but bringing them to a new place. We pray that we may be transformed and see beyond the suffering to the glory that Jesus promised.

- The reaction of Peter, James, and John was one of attraction and terror. There was the reassuring voice of the Father: 'This is my Son, the Beloved, listen to him!' Lord, you remind us of the glory you desire to share with us. May we have the faith to come down the mountain and continue the journey with you.

Monday 26 February
Luke 6:36–38

'Be merciful, just as your Father is merciful. Do not judge, and you will not be judged; do not condemn, and you will not be condemned. Forgive, and you will be forgiven; give, and it will be given to you. A good measure, pressed down, shaken together, running over, will be put into your lap; for the measure you give will be the measure you get back.'

- These days have been naming qualities of discipleship. Luke can be called the gospel of mercy, revealing a compassionate God who wants us to have the same care in our relationships. Lord, you are merciful to us and we pray that we may be tolerant and patient with the failings of others, as you are with ours.

- It is easy to fall into judgement and condemnation of those who seem to fall short of our standards. We are prone to fall into judgement of the personal aspects. May we have a humble stance that acknowledges our own limits so that we are more understanding of others.

Tuesday 27 February
Matthew 23:1–12

Then Jesus said to the crowds and to his disciples, 'The scribes and the Pharisees sit on Moses' seat; therefore, do whatever they teach you and follow it; but do not do as they do, for they do not practise what they teach. They tie up heavy burdens, hard to bear, and lay them on the shoulders of others; but they themselves are unwilling to lift a finger to move them. They do all their deeds to be seen by others; for they make their phylacteries broad and their fringes long. They love to have the place of honour at banquets and the best seats in the synagogues, and to be greeted with respect in the market-places, and to have people call them rabbi. But you are not to be called rabbi, for you have one teacher, and you are all students. And call no one your father on earth, for you have one Father—the one in heaven. Nor are you to be called instructors, for you have one instructor, the Messiah. The greatest among you will be your servant. All who exalt themselves will be humbled, and all who humble themselves will be exalted.'

• Moses had a prominent place in the faith story of the Israelites, as a teacher of the law. Those who succeeded him in that role, the scribes and the Pharisees, seemed to have lost perspective. Their outward behaviour was at odds with the spirit of the law. Lord, may we not be held bound by our own importance, but allow your teaching to show us the way.

- We live in a world where honours can take on much importance. Lord, your way is one of humility and truth. You bring down the powerful and raise up the lowly (Luke 1:52). Help us to transform our hearts to be more like yours, so that poverty, simplicity and truth are to the fore in our lives and in our relationships.

Wednesday 28 February
Matthew 20:17–28

While Jesus was going up to Jerusalem, he took the twelve disciples aside by themselves, and said to them on the way, 'See, we are going up to Jerusalem, and the Son of Man will be handed over to the chief priests and scribes, and they will condemn him to death; then they will hand him over to the Gentiles to be mocked and flogged and crucified; and on the third day he will be raised.'

Then the mother of the sons of Zebedee came to him with her sons, and kneeling before him, she asked a favour of him. And he said to her, 'What do you want?' She said to him, 'Declare that these two sons of mine will sit, one at your right hand and one at your left, in your kingdom.' But Jesus answered, 'You do not know what you are asking. Are you able to drink the cup that I am about to drink?' They said to him, 'We are able.' He said to them, 'You will indeed drink my cup, but to sit at my right hand and at my left, this is not mine to grant, but it is for those for whom it has been prepared by my Father.'

When the ten heard it, they were angry with the two brothers. But Jesus called them to him and said, 'You know that the rulers of the Gentiles lord it over them, and their great ones are tyrants over them. It will not be so among you; but whoever wishes to be great among you must be your servant, and whoever wishes to be first among you must be your slave; just as the Son of Man came not to be served but to serve, and to give his life a ransom for many.'

• Jesus made the journey to Jerusalem, foretelling what awaited him there. He would be 'handed over' to others. He wanted to do the Father's will. Lord, we desire to go to Jerusalem with you but are fearful of the cost and pain involved. Give us the strength to stay with you, for it is you we want, not suffering.

• This is another instance of the disciples not getting Jesus' message. The mother of James and John wanted some prominence for her sons. The other disciples had similar designs but were slower to take action. Jesus, give us your spirit of humility and service in our lives.

Thursday 29 February
Luke 16:19–31

Jesus said to them, 'There was a rich man who was dressed in purple and fine linen and who feasted sumptuously every day. And at his gate lay a poor man named Lazarus, covered with sores, who longed to satisfy his hunger with what fell from the rich man's table; even the dogs would come and lick his sores. The poor man died and was carried away by the angels to be with Abraham. The rich man also died and was buried. In Hades, where he was being tormented, he looked up and saw Abraham far away with Lazarus by his side. He called out, "Father Abraham, have mercy on me, and send Lazarus to dip the tip of his finger in water and cool my tongue; for I am in agony in these flames." But Abraham said, "Child, remember that during your lifetime you received your good things, and Lazarus in like manner evil things; but now he is comforted here, and you are in agony. Besides all this, between you and us a great chasm has been fixed, so that those who might want to pass from here to you cannot do so, and no one can cross from there to us." He said,

"Then, father, I beg you to send him to my father's house—for I have five brothers—that he may warn them, so that they will not also come into this place of torment." Abraham replied, "They have Moses and the prophets; they should listen to them." He said, "No, father Abraham; but if someone goes to them from the dead, they will repent." He said to him, "If they do not listen to Moses and the prophets, neither will they be convinced even if someone rises from the dead."'

- Another story of contrast, between a rich and a poor man. For Jesus, no one was excluded; he sought to nourish all with food that endured. It is an invitation to change our attitudes. May our poverty and a lack of inclusion not impede us in being voices for justice, seeking to bring about change.

- It is a world with unequal distribution of resources. While some dine well, others lack food. Jesus had a hunger for justice. This asks for action, not pious words. We pray that we may hunger for what is right and not remain silent at the gate of life.

Friday 1 March
Matthew 21:33–43, 45–46

Jesus said to them, 'Listen to another parable. There was a landowner who planted a vineyard, put a fence around it, dug a wine press in it, and built a watch-tower. Then he leased it to tenants and went to another country. When the harvest time had come, he sent his slaves to the tenants to collect his produce. But the tenants seized his slaves and beat one, killed another, and stoned another. Again he sent other slaves, more than the first; and they treated them in the same way. Finally he sent his son to them, saying, "They will respect my son." But when the tenants saw the son, they said to themselves, "This is the heir; come, let us kill him and get his inheritance." So they seized him, threw him out of the vineyard, and killed him. Now when the owner of the vineyard comes, what will he do to those tenants?' They said to him, 'He will put those wretches to a miserable death, and lease the vineyard to other tenants who will give him the produce at the harvest time.'

Jesus said to them, 'Have you never read in the scriptures:

> "The stone that the builders rejected
>   has become the cornerstone;
> this was the Lord's doing,
>   and it is amazing in our eyes"?

Therefore I tell you, the kingdom of God will be taken away from you and given to a people that pro-duces the fruits of the kingdom.'

When the chief priests and the Pharisees heard his parables, they realised that he was speaking about them. They wanted to arrest him, but they feared the crowds, because they regarded him as a prophet.

- Having made careful preparations, the landowner expected a good return. The self-interest of the tenants became apparent over time. Lord, help us to be responsible with the gifts given to us so that we produce a good harvest in your name.

- The owner sent his son, expecting that he would be given better treatment, but the tenants saw it as an opportunity. The story tells of the tenants coming to a miserable end, but could a compassionate God surprise us by acting differently? Lord, show us your compassion for the ways we have misused what you have entrusted to us.

Saturday 2 March
Luke 15:1–3, 11–32

Now all the tax-collectors and sinners were coming near to listen to him. And the Pharisees and the scribes were grumbling and saying, 'This fellow welcomes sinners and eats with them.'

So he told them this parable:

'There was a man who had two sons. The younger of them said to his father, "Father, give me the share of the property that will belong to me." So he divided his property between them. A few days later the younger son gathered all he had and travelled to a distant country, and there he squandered his property in dissolute living. When he had spent everything, a severe famine took place throughout that country, and he began to be in need. So he went and hired himself out to one of the citizens of that country, who sent him to his fields to feed the pigs. He would gladly have filled himself with the pods that the pigs were eating; and no one gave him anything. But when he came to himself he said, "How many of my father's hired hands have bread enough and to spare, but here I am dying of hunger! I will get up and go to my father, and I will say to him, 'Father, I have sinned against heaven and before you; I am no longer worthy to be called your son; treat me like one of your hired hands.'" So he set off and went to his father. But while he was still far off, his father saw him and was filled with compassion; he ran and put his arms around him and kissed him. Then the son said to him, "Father, I have sinned against heaven and before you; I am no longer worthy to be called your son." But the father said to his slaves, "Quickly, bring out a robe—the best one—and put it on him; put a ring on his finger and sandals on his feet. And get the fatted calf and kill it, and let us eat and celebrate; for this son of mine was dead and is alive again; he was lost and is found!" And they began to celebrate.

'Now his elder son was in the field; and when he came and approached the house, he heard music and dancing. He called one of the slaves and asked what was going on. He replied, "Your brother has come, and your father has killed the fatted calf, because he has got him back safe and sound." Then he became angry and refused to go in. His father came out and began to plead with him. But he answered his father, "Listen! For all these years I have been working like a slave for you, and I have never disobeyed your command; yet you have never given me even a young goat so that I might celebrate with my friends. But when this son of yours came back, who has devoured your property with prostitutes, you killed the fatted calf for him!" Then the father said to him, "Son, you are always with me, and all that is mine is yours. But we had to celebrate and rejoice, because this brother of yours was dead and has come to life; he was lost and has been found."'

- A familiar parable of contrasts. The younger son asked for freedom and went far away to get distance from home. In time, he 'came to himself' and decided to return. May we recognise when we wander away so that we may come to our senses and return home to you.

- This is one of the great stories of compassion, which means being moved to the depth of one's being. The father reached out to his errant son, restoring him to full family membership. We pray that we may recognise our need and welcome the extravagant, forgiving love of the Father.

3–9 March 2024

Something to think and pray about each day this week:

In Italian, Lent is *quaresima* or forty (days). In German, it is *Fastenzeit*, literally 'fasting time', or time for bodily restraint. Our English word comes from an older Anglo-Saxon word for spring—len(c)ten—whence our word Lent, as the days are lengthening. Thus, Italian tells us *how long it will last* (with its symbolic overtones). German tells us *what we are supposed to do* in that season. But English tells us *what is supposed to happen*, that is, we hope to experience a springtime of faith, a time of growth and new life.

Ask the LORD for rain in the season of the late spring rains—the LORD who causes thunderstorms—and he will give everyone showers of rain and green growth in the field. (Zechariah 10:1)

Kieran J. O'Mahony OSA,
Hearers of the Word: Praying and Exploring the Readings for Lent and Holy Week

The Presence of God

I remind myself that, as I sit here now, God is gazing on me with love and holding me in being. I pause for a moment and think of this.

Freedom

'There are very few people who realise what God would make of them if they abandoned themselves into his hands, and let themselves be formed by his grace' (St Ignatius). I ask for the grace to trust myself totally to God's love.

Consciousness

Where do I sense hope, encouragement and growth in my life? By looking back over the past few months, I may be able to see which activities and occasions have produced rich fruit. If I do notice such areas, I will determine to give those areas both time and space in the future.

The Word

Lord Jesus, you became human to communicate with me. You walked and worked on this earth. You endured the heat and struggled with the cold. All your time on this earth was spent in caring for humanity. You healed the sick, you raised the dead. Most important of all, you saved me from death.

(Please turn to the Scripture on the following pages. Inspiration points are there, should you need them. When you are ready, return here to continue.)

Conversation

What is stirring in me as I pray? Am I consoled, troubled, left cold? I imagine Jesus standing or sitting at my side, and I share my feelings with him.

Conclusion

Glory be to the Father, and to the Son, and to the Holy Spirit, as it was in the beginning, is now and ever shall be, world without end. Amen.

Sunday 3 March
Third Sunday of Lent

John 2:13–25

The Passover of the Jews was near, and Jesus went up to Jerusalem. In the temple he found people selling cattle, sheep, and doves, and the money-changers seated at their tables. Making a whip of cords, he drove all of them out of the temple, both the sheep and the cattle. He also poured out the coins of the money-changers and overturned their tables. He told those who were selling the doves, 'Take these things out of here! Stop making my Father's house a market-place!' His disciples remembered that it was written, 'Zeal for your house will consume me.' The Jews then said to him, 'What sign can you show us for doing this?' Jesus answered them, 'Destroy this temple, and in three days I will raise it up.' The Jews then said, 'This temple has been under construction for forty-six years, and will you raise it up in three days?' But he was speaking of the temple of his body. After he was raised from the dead, his disciples remembered that he had said this; and they believed the scripture and the word that Jesus had spoken.

When he was in Jerusalem during the Passover festival, many believed in his name because they saw the signs that he was doing. But Jesus on his part would not entrust himself to them, because he knew all people and needed no one to testify about anyone; for he himself knew what was in everyone.

- The Gospel of John is attentive to the Jewish festivals and their place in the lives of the people. What Jesus observed was at variance with what he believed about his Father's house. May we, who live in the market-place that has become a temple for many, have the courage and zeal to stand for the truth.

- Jesus declared a different mission in the sacred environment of the Temple. He spoke of himself as the new temple. Lord, help us to see beyond structures and buildings to the person of Jesus as the cornerstone of our faith.

Monday 4 March
Luke 4:24–30

And he said, 'Truly I tell you, no prophet is accepted in the prophet's hometown. But the truth is, there were many widows in Israel in the time of Elijah, when the heaven was shut up three years and six months, and there was a severe famine over all the land; yet Elijah was sent to none of them except to a widow at Zarephath in Sidon. There were also many lepers in Israel in the time of the prophet Elisha, and none of them was cleansed except Naaman the Syrian.' When they heard this, all in the synagogue were filled with rage. They got up, drove him out of the town, and led him to the brow of the hill on which their town was built, so that they might hurl him off the cliff. But he passed through the midst of them and went on his way.

- Jesus' reputation had grown when he returned home. His personal approach evoked a strong reaction. The local people thought he was to blame for their discomfort. Help us to realise when we fall into the trap of confusing the message with the messenger, so that we may allow the truth to change us.

- Jesus drew on the example of outsiders, who responded to the message of the prophets. He was calling his hearers to faith in him. Lord, help us to recognise that we are the locals who are slow to accept you, as our prejudices can blind us to who you really are.

Tuesday 5 March
Matthew 18:21–35

Then Peter came and said to him, 'Lord, if another member of the church sins against me, how often should I forgive? As many as seven times?' Jesus said to him, 'Not seven times, but, I tell you, seventy-seven times.

'For this reason the kingdom of heaven may be compared to a king who wished to settle accounts with his slaves. When he began the reckoning, one who owed him ten thousand talents was brought to him; and, as he could not pay, his lord ordered him to be sold, together with his wife and children and all his possessions, and payment to be made. So the slave fell on his knees before him, saying, "Have patience with me, and I will pay you everything." And out of pity for him, the lord of that slave released him and forgave him the debt. But that same slave, as he went out, came upon one of his fellow-slaves who owed him a hundred denarii; and seizing him by the throat, he said, "Pay what you owe." Then his fellow-slave fell down and pleaded with him, "Have patience with me, and I will pay you." But he refused; then he went and threw him into prison until he should pay the debt. When his fellow-slaves saw what had happened, they were greatly distressed, and they went and reported to their lord all that had taken place. Then his lord summoned him and said to him, "You wicked slave! I forgave you all that debt because you pleaded with me. Should you not have had mercy on your fellow-slave, as I had mercy on you?" And in anger his lord handed him over to be tortured until he should pay his entire debt. So my heavenly Father will also do to every one of you, if you do not forgive your brother or sister from your heart.'

- Peter asked Jesus a practical question about the number of times to forgive. Jesus was thinking of more than limited numbers. Jesus, you reveal a merciful God of love who forgives without limit;

open our hearts to have a similar disposition when we feel hurt or overlooked.

- Jesus taught and lived forgiveness. In life, small-mindedness and a lack of perspective can prevail. Forgiveness is key to the quality of family and community life. Lord, help us to appreciate your forgiveness so that we can have larger hearts in the situations of conflict that we encounter in life.

Wednesday 6 March
Matthew 5:17–19

Jesus said to them, 'Do not think that I have come to abolish the law or the prophets; I have come not to abolish but to fulfil. For truly I tell you, until heaven and earth pass away, not one letter, not one stroke of a letter, will pass from the law until all is accomplished. Therefore, whoever breaks one of the least of these commandments, and teaches others to do the same, will be called least in the kingdom of heaven; but whoever does them and teaches them will be called great in the kingdom of heaven.'

- The law of God, given to Moses, and the teaching of the prophets were important aspects of the lives of the Israelites as people of the covenant. Lord, as people of the new covenant, may we be guided by your law of love in living as your disciples.

- Jesus came to fulfil the law and the prophets, bringing the people to a new place in a relationship of love with him. The law is to be written on our hearts, not on stone tablets. May we grow in freedom to live out our relationship with Jesus and to be prophetic voices for the truth he reveals to us.

Thursday 7 March
Luke 11:14–23

Now he was casting out a demon that was mute; when the demon had gone out, the one who had been mute spoke, and the crowds were amazed. But some of them said, 'He casts out demons by Beelzebul, the ruler of the demons.' Others, to test him, kept demanding from him a sign from heaven. But he knew what they were thinking and said to them, 'Every kingdom divided against itself becomes a desert, and house falls on house. If Satan also is divided against himself, how will his kingdom stand?—for you say that I cast out the demons by Beelzebul. Now if I cast out the demons by Beelzebul, by whom do your exorcists cast them out? Therefore they will be your judges. But if it is by the finger of God that I cast out the demons, then the kingdom of God has come to you. When a strong man, fully armed, guards his castle, his property is safe. But when one stronger than he attacks him and overpowers him, he takes away his armour in which he trusted and divides his plunder. Whoever is not with me is against me, and whoever does not gather with me scatters.'

- Jesus preached and taught. Healing added a further dimension to his ministry of transformation. We sometimes seem to lack the power of speech when we meet an inhospitable audience. May we have the courage to proclaim Jesus and bring his healing to the broken people of our time.

- Jesus cast out demons by the power of God. His kingdom is one of justice, love and peace. We are called as his companions to stand by him, being a source of unity. Lord, may we draw strength from you, knowing that your power is greater than the voices of dissent and the forces of evil.

Friday 8 March
Mark 12:28–34

One of the scribes came near and heard them disputing with one another, and seeing that he answered them well, he asked him, 'Which commandment is the first of all?' Jesus answered, 'The first is, "Hear, O Israel: the Lord our God, the Lord is one; you shall love the Lord your God with all your heart, and with all your soul, and with all your mind, and with all your strength." The second is this, "You shall love your neighbour as yourself." There is no other commandment greater than these.' Then the scribe said to him,

'You are right, Teacher; you have truly said that "he is one, and besides him there is no other"; and "to love him with all the heart, and with all the understanding, and with all the strength", and "to love one's neighbour as oneself",—this is much more important than all whole burnt-offerings and sacrifices.' When Jesus saw that he answered wisely, he said to him, 'You are not far from the kingdom of God.' After that no one dared to ask him any question.

- The Ten Commandments are far more than a series of negative prescriptions, of 'Thou shalt not'. They provide a way of life, founded on love, to right relationships with God and others. May we value more fully the guidance that God gives us and allow it to enrich our lives and our relationships.

- In responding to the scribe, Jesus gave a nice summary in saying that loving God was first and loving others followed from it. Love was at the heart of God's way. Lord, give us hearts that love you and others as our brothers and sisters whom you love unconditionally.

Saturday 9 March
Luke 18:9–14

He also told this parable to some who trusted in themselves that they were righteous and regarded others with contempt: 'Two men went up to the temple to pray, one a Pharisee and the other a tax-collector. The

Pharisee, standing by himself, was praying thus, "God, I thank you that I am not like other people: thieves, rogues, adulterers, or even like this tax-collector. I fast twice a week; I give a tenth of all my income." But the tax-collector, standing far off, would not even look up to heaven, but was beating his breast and saying, "God, be merciful to me, a sinner!" I tell you, this man went down to his home justified rather than the other; for all who exalt themselves will be humbled, but all who humble themselves will be exalted.'

- This is another story of contrasting attitudes. How the Pharisee and tax collector saw themselves and God influenced how they prayed. May we have the freedom to acknowledge the truth about God and ourselves so that we may pray in humility for mercy.

- We are halfway through Lent and this is a time to check how we are doing. We began centred on God, but that may have shifted. Perhaps we are proud of how well we are doing or critical of our shortcomings. Lord, help us to renew our focus and to keep our eyes on you as we continue our Lenten journey.

The Fourth Week of Lent
10–16 March 2024

Something to think and pray about each day this week:

In preparing for Lent, Pope Francis quotes Hosea (6:6): 'What I want is mercy, not sacrifice'. This is a shift of emphasis away from what I do, to what God does in me.

Yet people may still get caught up in Lent as simply a time of self-sacrifice, a giving up of stuff through self-discipline or willpower. There's nothing wrong with that, but just notice the emphasis on the self and what 'I' am doing. It seems almost to cut God out of the picture.

The quote from Hosea is inviting us to act in a merciful or loving way, which is subtly different. For example, a person may be called to go the extra mile with someone, to mend a fractured relationship, to ask forgiveness for a hurt caused, to turn away from vice and reform their life.

Obviously there is sacrifice involved here, and there is always a cost in changing for the better, but the goal is not sacrifice, it's trying to do the right thing, the loving thing, and it can be hard . . . doing what God wants, though, brings its own courage, hidden strength and grace, which allows us to go beyond our normal selves.

Brendan McManus SJ,
The Sacred Heart Messenger, February 2021

The Presence of God

I pause for a moment and reflect on God's life-giving presence in every part of my body, in everything around me, in the whole of my life.

Freedom

Many countries are at this moment suffering the agonies of war. I bow my head in thanksgiving for my freedom. I pray for all prisoners and captives.

Consciousness

Knowing that God loves me unconditionally, I look honestly over the past day, its events and my feelings. Do I have something to be grateful for? Then I give thanks. Is there something I am sorry for? Then I ask forgiveness.

The Word

Now I turn to the Scripture set out for me this day. I read slowly over the words and see if any sentence or sentiment appeals to me. *(Please turn to the Scripture on the following pages. Inspiration points are there, should you need them. When you are ready, return here to continue.)*

Conversation

I know with certainty that there were times when you carried me, Lord. There were times when it was through your strength that I got through the dark times in my life.

Conclusion
Glory be to the Father, and to the Son, and to the Holy Spirit, as it was in the beginning, is now and ever shall be, world without end. Amen.

Sunday 10 March
Fourth Sunday of Lent

John 3:14–21

'And just as Moses lifted up the serpent in the wilderness, so must the Son of Man be lifted up, that whoever believes in him may have eternal life.

'For God so loved the world that he gave his only Son, so that everyone who believes in him may not perish but may have eternal life.

'Indeed, God did not send the Son into the world to condemn the world, but in order that the world might be saved through him. Those who believe in him are not condemned; but those who do not believe are condemned already, because they have not believed in the name of the only Son of God. And this is the judgement, that the light has come into the world, and people loved darkness rather than light because their deeds were evil. For all who do evil hate the light and do not come to the light, so that their deeds may not be exposed. But those who do what is true come to the light, so that it may be clearly seen that their deeds have been done in God.'

- Jesus was sent into the world to bring salvation. The world is ambivalent to Jesus, though God's desire is clear—for us to have eternal life though Jesus. We pray to recognise the gift and the desire of God so that we are not captivated and drawn off course by the attractions of the world.

- The lifting up of the serpent brought liberation to the Israelites from its poisonous effects (Numbers 21:9). Jesus was to be lifted up on the cross, offering his life for our salvation. As children of light may we have hearts that believe in Jesus and respond in love, raising up people who are caught in the darkness.

Monday 11 March

John 4:43–54

When the two days were over, he went from that place to Galilee (for Jesus himself had testified that a prophet has no honour in the prophet's own country). When he came to Galilee, the Galileans welcomed him, since they had seen all that he had done in Jerusalem at the festival; for they too had gone to the festival.

Then he came again to Cana in Galilee where he had changed the water into wine. Now there was a royal official whose son lay ill in Capernaum. When he heard that Jesus had come from Judea to Galilee, he went and begged him to come down and heal his son, for he was at the point of death. Then Jesus said to him, 'Unless you see signs and wonders you will not believe.' The official said to him, 'Sir, come down before my little boy dies.' Jesus said to him, 'Go; your son will live.' The man believed the word that Jesus spoke to him and started on his way. As he was going down, his slaves met him and told him that his child was alive. So he asked them the hour when he began to recover, and they said to him, 'Yesterday at one in the afternoon the fever left him.' The father realised that this was the hour when Jesus had said to him, 'Your son will live.' So he himself believed, along with his whole household. Now this was the second sign that Jesus did after coming from Judea to Galilee.

- Jesus, as a prophet, was welcomed in Galilee by the people who had seen what he had done in Jerusalem at the festival. Evidence had been provided to enable them to move on. Lord, may we have the faith to accept the evidence you give and to value others as your people.

- A royal official, believing Jesus could heal his son, begged for it. Jesus challenged the official's faith before responding. We pray to recognise the wonders the Lord performs so that our faith is deepened and our response is more wholehearted.

Tuesday 12 March
John 5:1–16

After this there was a festival of the Jews, and Jesus went up to Jerusalem.

Now in Jerusalem by the Sheep Gate there is a pool, called in Hebrew Beth-zatha, which has five porticoes. In these lay many invalids—blind, lame, and paralysed. One man was there who had been ill for thirty-eight years. When Jesus saw him lying there and knew that he had been there a long time, he said to him, 'Do you want to be made well?' The sick man answered him, 'Sir, I have no one to put me into the pool when the water is stirred up; and while I am making my way, someone else steps down ahead of me.' Jesus said to him, 'Stand up, take your mat and walk.' At once the man was made well, and he took up his mat and began to walk.

Now that day was a sabbath. So the Jews said to the man who had been cured, 'It is the sabbath; it is not lawful for you to carry your mat.' But he answered them, 'The man who made me well said to me, "Take up your mat and walk."' They asked him, 'Who is the man who said to you, "Take it up and walk"?' Now the man who had been healed did not know who it was, for Jesus had disappeared in the crowd that was there. Later Jesus found him in the temple and said to him, 'See, you have been made well! Do not sin any more, so that nothing worse happens to you.' The man went away and told the Jews that it was Jesus who had made him well. Therefore the Jews started persecuting Jesus, because he was doing such things on the sabbath.

- Jesus was present at another festival and healed on the sabbath. He was Lord of the sabbath as well as being the new temple. Lord, help us to appreciate external places and occasions of worship, that we may develop the interior dimensions that enhance them.

- Jesus healed the man who had been ill for a long time. The Jews seemed to be more concerned about externals, such as carrying a mat, whereas Jesus was compassionate and personal. Doing God's work aroused opposition on this occasion. May we be guided by the spirit and not the letter of the law in helping others.

Wednesday 13 March

John 5:17–30

But Jesus answered them, 'My Father is still working, and I also am working.' For this reason the Jews were seeking all the more to kill him, because he was not only breaking the sabbath, but was also calling God his own Father, thereby making himself equal to God.

Jesus said to them, 'Very truly, I tell you, the Son can do nothing on his own, but only what he sees the Father doing; for whatever the Father does, the Son does likewise. The Father loves the Son and shows him all that he himself is doing; and he will show him greater works than these, so that you will be astonished. Indeed, just as the Father raises the dead and gives them life, so also the Son gives life to whomsoever he wishes. The Father judges no one but has given all judgement to the Son, so that all may honour the Son just as they honour the Father. Anyone who does not honour the Son does not honour the Father who sent him. Very truly, I tell you, anyone who hears my word and believes him who sent me has eternal life, and does not come under judgement, but has passed from death to life.

'Very truly, I tell you, the hour is coming, and is now here, when the dead will hear the voice of the Son of God, and those who hear will live. For just as the Father has life in himself, so he has granted the Son also to have life in himself; and he has given him authority to execute judgement, because he is the Son of Man. Do not be astonished at this; for the hour is coming when all who are in their graves will hear his voice and will come out—those who have done good, to the resurrection of life, and those who have done evil, to the resurrection of condemnation.

'I can do nothing on my own. As I hear, I judge; and my judgement is just, because I seek to do not my own will but the will of him who sent me.'

- Our God is active and close to us. Jesus said, 'My Father is still working, and I also am working.' Jesus is Emmanuel, God with us. In the joys and struggles of life may we draw strength and comfort from the presence of Jesus and the work he has done for us.

- Jesus was one with the Father in his life and mission. He draws us into this relationship of love. Having eternal life speaks of life now and not just in the future. Lord, help us to come to a deeper faith in your presence with us and within us, that we may share your glory.

Thursday 14 March

John 5:31–47

Jesus said to them, 'If I testify about myself, my testimony is not true. There is another who testifies on my behalf, and I know that his testimony to me is true. You sent messengers to John, and he testified to the truth. Not that I accept such human testimony, but I say these things so that you may be saved. He was a burning and shining lamp, and you were willing to rejoice for a while in his light. But I have a testimony greater than John's. The works that the Father has given me to complete, the very works that I am doing, testify on my behalf that the Father has sent me. And the Father who sent me has himself testified on my behalf. You have never heard his voice or seen his form, and you do not have his word abiding in you, because you do not believe him whom he has sent.

'You search the scriptures because you think that in them you have eternal life; and it is they that testify on my behalf. Yet you refuse to come to me to have life. I do not accept glory from human beings. But I know that you do not have the love of God in you. I have come in my Father's name, and you do not accept me; if another comes in his own name, you will accept him. How can you believe when you accept glory from one another and do not seek the glory that comes from the one who alone is God? Do not think that I will accuse you before the Father; your accuser is Moses, on whom you have set your hope. If you believed Moses, you would believe me, for he wrote about me. But if you do not believe what he wrote, how will you believe what I say?'

- The will of the Father and being sent was of central importance in the life and mission of Jesus. He said, 'I seek not to do my own will but the will of him who sent me.' May we who are sent by him have the freedom to carry out what the Lord wants in our lives of service.

- The identity of Jesus was becoming clearer over time. Jesus called on witnesses to testify to his identity—John the Baptist, the Father, the works he did, Scripture and Moses. We pray that we may have the faith and wisdom to notice the many signs that Jesus shares with us so that we are more effective witnesses for him.

Friday 15 March
John 7:1–2, 10, 25–30

After this Jesus went about in Galilee. He did not wish to go about in Judea because the Jews were looking for an opportunity to kill him. Now the Jewish festival of Booths was near.

But after his brothers had gone to the festival, then he also went, not publicly but as it were in secret.

Now some of the people of Jerusalem were saying, 'Is not this the man whom they are trying to kill? And here he is, speaking openly, but they say nothing to him! Can it be that the authorities really know that this is the Messiah? Yet we know where this man is from; but when the Messiah comes, no one will know where he is from.' Then Jesus cried out as he was teaching in the temple, 'You know me, and you know where I am from. I have not come on my own. But the one who sent me is true, and you do not know him. I know him, because I am from him, and he sent me.' Then they tried to arrest him, but no one laid hands on him, because his hour had not yet come.

- Jesus went back to Galilee, but he went to Jerusalem secretly for the festival, which gave thanks for the harvest as well as recalled a time when the chosen people lived in tents. Lord, may we draw strength from you and honour your festivals on the journey of life.

- There was conflict between knowing Jesus and knowing about him. His background and teaching led to divided opinions. Lord, we live at a time when many do not believe in you or see you as relevant. We pray that we may know you better and give more personal testimony to you.

Saturday 16 March

John 7:40–53

When they heard these words, some in the crowd said, 'This is really the prophet.' Others said, 'This is the Messiah.' But some asked, 'Surely the Messiah does not come from Galilee, does he? Has not the scripture said that the Messiah is descended from David and comes from Bethlehem, the village where David lived?' So there was a division in the crowd because of him. Some of them wanted to arrest him, but no one laid hands on him.

Then the temple police went back to the chief priests and Pharisees, who asked them, 'Why did you not arrest him?' The police answered, 'Never has anyone spoken like this!' Then the Pharisees replied, 'Surely you have not been deceived too, have you? Has any one of the authorities or of the Pharisees believed in him? But this crowd, which does not know the law—they are accursed.' Nicodemus, who had gone to Jesus before, and who was one of them, asked, 'Our law does not judge people without first giving them a hearing to find out what they are doing, does it?' They replied, 'Surely you are not also from Galilee, are you? Search and you will see that no prophet is to arise from Galilee.'

- There were more disputes about who Jesus was. Concerns at the practical level about his background blinded the crowd to the true message of Jesus. May we have a deeper sense of who Jesus is and a closer relationship with him so that we can make him known.

- There were divided opinions on Jesus. The temple police failed to arrest him, to the unhappiness of the chief priests and the Pharisees. Nicodemus, who had first come to Jesus by night (John 3:2), said Jesus was entitled to a fair hearing. Lord, you present reliable credentials. May we have the courage to declare this.

The Fifth Week of Lent
17–23 March 2024

Something to think and pray about each day this week:

Our stories of St Patrick are varied. Legend puts him in the corner of countless fields the length and breadth of Ireland. It puts him on top of Croagh Patrick, in the stillness of Lough Derg and at numerous holy wells. Was he in these places? The answer may very well be yes—he was there insofar as his name and the flame from Slane reflected the Gospel and shone in the hearts and souls of Irish people.

Is he in parades, marching bands or floats? Is he in greened rivers or landmarks across the globe that are, for the day, illuminated in green? He could and should be, but he might struggle to be found in many of the practices associated with him today.

It is about keeping the flame alive and burning and finding him again, in the corner of a field, in the lovely church with its towering steeple, in the quiet home where the 'Rosary is told', in the holy water font inside the front door of a house where blessing is made possible as we come and go.

Vincent Sherlock, *The Sacred Heart Messenger*,
March 2022

The Presence of God

I pause for a moment and think of the love and the grace that God showers on me. I am created in the image and likeness of God; I am God's dwelling place.

Freedom

Lord, you granted me the great gift of freedom. In these times, O Lord, grant that I may be free from any form of racism or intolerance. Remind me that we are all equal in your loving eyes.

Consciousness

Knowing that God loves me unconditionally, I can afford to be honest about how I am.
How has the day been, and how do I feel now? I share my feelings openly with the Lord.

The Word

I take my time to read the word of God slowly, a few times, allowing myself to dwell on anything that strikes me. *(Please turn to the Scripture on the following pages. Inspiration points are there, should you need them. When you are ready, return here to continue.)*

Conversation

Sometimes I wonder what I might say if I were to meet you in person, Lord.

I think I might say, 'Thank you', because you are always there for me.

Conclusion
I thank God for these moments we have spent together and for any insights I have been given concerning the text.

Sunday 17 March
Fifth Sunday of Lent
St Patrick, Patron of Ireland
Mark 16:15–20

And he said to them, 'Go into all the world and proclaim the good news to the whole creation. The one who believes and is baptised will be saved; but the one who does not believe will be condemned. And these signs will accompany those who believe: by using my name they will cast out demons; they will speak in new tongues; they will pick up snakes in their hands, and if they drink any deadly thing, it will not hurt them; they will lay their hands on the sick, and they will recover.'

So then the Lord Jesus, after he had spoken to them, was taken up into heaven and sat down at the right hand of God. And they went out and proclaimed the good news everywhere, while the Lord worked with them and confirmed the message by the signs that accompanied it.

- Jesus drew Patrick to himself and sent him on mission to Ireland. It meant returning to a place where he had been enslaved and had suffered. Help us to recognise where we are enslaved now so that we might be free to announce the good news as Patrick did.

- The surprising ways of God bore fruit through the labours of St Patrick, who came to a pagan nation.

There is need of a renewed vision to declare that mission in a changed country. May we value the gifts of the past and be strengthened by them in facing the future.

Monday 18 March

John 8:2–11

Early in the morning he came again to the temple. All the people came to him and he sat down and began to teach them. The scribes and the Pharisees brought a woman who had been caught in adultery; and making her stand before all of them, they said to him, 'Teacher, this woman was caught in the very act of committing adultery. Now in the law Moses commanded us to stone such women. Now what do you say?' They said this to test him, so that they might have some charge to bring against him. Jesus bent down and wrote with his finger on the ground. When they kept on questioning him, he straightened up and said to them, 'Let anyone among you who is without sin be the first to throw a stone at her.' And once again he bent down and wrote on the ground. When they heard it, they went away, one by one, beginning with the elders; and Jesus was left alone with the woman standing before him. Jesus straightened up and said to her, 'Woman, where are they? Has no one condemned you?' She said, 'No one, sir.'

And Jesus said, 'Neither do I condemn you. Go your way, and from now on do not sin again.'

- In the sacred setting of the temple, the Pharisees challenged Jesus. A woman was accused of adultery. The Pharisees were asked to look into their own hearts, at the hidden stones they were carrying. Lord, help us to appreciate the dignity of all sinners, knowing that we are included.

- The Pharisees asked a practical question about the law. Jesus saw beyond the law to a person. He did not focus on the past, but offered a new future. Lord, may we be able to straighten up, look you in the eye and accept your forgiveness.

Tuesday 19 March
St Joseph,
Husband of the Blessed Virgin Mary
Luke 2:41–51

Now every year his parents went to Jerusalem for the festival of the Passover. And when he was twelve years old, they went up as usual for the festival. When the festival was ended and they started to return, the boy Jesus stayed behind in Jerusalem, but his parents did not know it. Assuming that he was in the group of travellers, they went a day's journey. Then they started to look for him among their relatives and friends. When they did not find him, they returned to Jerusalem to search for him. After three days they found him in the temple, sitting among the teachers, listening to them and asking them questions. And all who heard him were amazed at his understanding and his answers. When his parents saw him they were astonished; and his mother said to him, 'Child, why have you treated us like this? Look, your father and I have been searching for you in great anxiety.' He said to them, 'Why were you searching for me? Did you not know that I must be in my Father's house?' But they did not understand what he said to them. Then he went down with them and came to Nazareth, and was obedient to them. His mother treasured all these things in her heart.

- Joseph was described as 'righteous' (Matthew 1:19). He went with Mary and Jesus to the Temple in Jerusalem for the Passover. Faith and trust in God were evident in his life. May we imitate him by manifesting our faith in the ordinary and the everyday.

- With Mary, Joseph searched for Jesus when he was lost. It was challenging for Joseph to understand Jesus' reply about being in the Father's house. Lord, may we draw strength from Joseph's searching, that we may take Jesus home with us.

Wednesday 20 March

John 8:31–42

Then Jesus said to the Jews who had believed in him, 'If you continue in my word, you are truly my disciples; and you will know the truth, and the truth will make you free.' They answered him, 'We are descendants of Abraham and have never been slaves to anyone. What do you mean by saying, "You will be made free"?'

Jesus answered them, 'Very truly, I tell you, everyone who commits sin is a slave to sin. The slave does not have a permanent place in the household; the son has a place there for ever. So if the Son makes you free, you will be free indeed. I know that you are descendants of Abraham; yet you look for an opportunity to kill me, because there is no place in you for my word. I declare what I have seen in the Father's presence; as for you, you should do what you have heard from the Father.'

They answered him, 'Abraham is our father.' Jesus said to them, 'If you were Abraham's children, you would be doing what Abraham did, but now you are trying to kill me, a man who has told you the truth that I heard from God. This is not what Abraham did. You are indeed doing what your father does.' They said to him, 'We are not illegitimate children; we have one father, God himself.' Jesus said to them, 'If God were your Father, you would love me, for I came from God and now I am here. I did not come on my own, but he sent me.'

- Jesus told and lived the truth of who he was and shared the Father's message with us. The truth liberates, taking away all disguises and pretence. Lord, help us to acknowledge and accept the truth of who you are and who we are, so that our relationship with you is more real.

- Jesus is the Son who sets us free and desires us to respond to that gift. He came into the world to testify to the truth and those who belong to the truth listen to his voice. Lord, may we have the freedom to hear your truth and let it guide our lives.

Thursday 21 March
John 8:51–59

Jesus said to them, 'Very truly, I tell you, whoever keeps my word will never see death.' The Jews said to him, 'Now we know that you have a demon. Abraham died, and so did the prophets; yet you say, "Whoever keeps my word will never taste death." Are you greater than our father Abraham, who died? The prophets also died. Who do you claim to be?' Jesus answered, 'If I glorify myself, my glory is nothing. It is my Father who glorifies me, he of whom you say, "He is our God", though you do not know him. But I know him; if I were to say that I do not know him,

I would be a liar like you. But I do know him and I keep his word. Your ancestor Abraham rejoiced that he would see my day; he saw it and was glad.' Then the Jews said to him, 'You are not yet fifty years old, and have you seen Abraham?' Jesus said to them, 'Very truly, I tell you, before Abraham was, I am.' So they picked up stones to throw at him, but Jesus hid himself and went out of the temple.

• Jesus' word was life-giving. His hearers were trapped at the surface level so they could not hear it. Lord, help us to retain your vision amid the many voices that clamour for attention, being focused more on the immediate than the enduring.

• Jesus' claim of knowing and being at one with the Father brought much confusion and downright opposition, with a desire to kill him. We pray to be drawn more fully into that love relationship with the Father that will guide us through the discordant voices of this age.

Friday 22 March
John 10:31–42

The Jews took up stones again to stone him. Jesus replied, 'I have shown you many good works from the Father. For which of these are you going to stone me?' The Jews answered, 'It is not for a good work that we are going to stone you, but for blasphemy, because you, though only a human being, are making yourself God.' Jesus answered, 'Is it not written in your law, "I said, you are gods"? If those to whom the word of God came were called "gods"—and the scripture cannot be annulled—can you say that the one whom the Father has sanctified and sent into the world is blaspheming because I said, "I am God's Son"? If I am not doing the works of my Father, then do not believe me. But if I do them, even though you do not believe me, believe the works, so that you may know and understand that the Father is in me and I am in the Father.' Then they tried to arrest him again, but he escaped from their hands.

He went away again across the Jordan to the place where John had been baptising earlier, and he remained there. Many came to him, and they were saying, 'John performed no sign, but everything that John said about this man was true.' And many believed in him there.

- The build-up of opposition became more evident, with Jesus seen as the problem. He was accused of making himself God. We ask that we may appreciate him more fully, being invited to share in his divinity as he shared in our humanity.

- They tried to arrest Jesus but he escaped their hands. Some came to believe in him as they were able to interpret the signs. May we have that facility and the freedom to recognise and to declare that we believe in him.

Saturday 23 March
John 11:45–56

Many of the Jews therefore, who had come with Mary and had seen what Jesus did, believed in him. But some of them went to the Pharisees and told them what he had done. So the chief priests and the Pharisees called a meeting of the council, and said, 'What are we to do? This man is performing many signs. If we let him go on like this, everyone will believe in him, and the Romans will come and destroy both our holy place and our nation.' But one of them, Caiaphas, who was high priest that year, said to them, 'You know nothing at all! You do not understand that it is better for you to have one man die for the people than to have the whole nation destroyed.' He did not say this on his own, but being high priest that year he prophesied that Jesus was about to die for the nation, and not for the nation only, but to gather into one the dispersed children of God. So from that day on they planned to put him to death.

Jesus therefore no longer walked about openly among the Jews, but went from there to a town called Ephraim in the region near the wilderness; and he remained there with the disciples.

Now the Passover of the Jews was near, and many went up from the country to Jerusalem before the Passover to purify themselves. They were looking for Jesus and were asking one another as they stood in the temple, 'What do you think? Surely he will not come to the festival, will he?'

- The religious leaders were becoming more perturbed by reports about Jesus. Caiaphas said it was better to have one man die for the people than to have the whole nation destroyed. Lord, deepen our faith to see your death as the way to life and the formation of a new nation.

- The Passover was near, but Jesus was about to initiate a new Passover that would bring deliverance from internal slavery. He did not go about openly because of the opposition. Lord, give us the freedom to tell where you are to be found, as we need your help to bring people to you, the source of life.

24–30 March 2024

Something to think and pray about each day this week:

On Palm Sunday the Teacher says, 'I am to celebrate the Passover with you.' He enters each of our homes and turns them into churches; and, even more, present in each place, lifted on the cross of his own human life—'and I, if I be lifted up, will draw all things to myself' (John 12:32, cf. 3:14, 5:21). He unites us all together in one body. It is this body of Christ, each other and the world, that we receive on Palm Sunday—this is our global eucharist: bearing each other's burdens, aware of the world's suffering.

Palm Sunday also takes us to the cross. Symbols give us our identity, self-image, our way of explaining ourselves to ourselves and to others. Symbols determine the kind of history we tell and retell. In the Christian tradition the cross is the ultimate symbol. Today this cross remains as a poignant, and appropriate, reminder of a man who embodied the Christian virtue of loving without counting the cost, and who tragically paid the ultimate price. Through this cross a man long dead lives again, somehow speaking to ears that belong to people not yet born.

John Scally,
The Sacred Heart Messenger, April 2021

The Presence of God

Dear Jesus, today I call on you, but not to ask for anything. I'd like only to dwell in your presence. May my heart respond to your love.

Freedom

God, my creator, you gave me life and the gift of freedom. Through your love I exist in this world. May I never take the gift of life for granted. May I always respect others' right to life.

Consciousness

I ask how I am today. Am I particularly tired, stressed or anxious? If any of these characteristics apply, can I try to let go of the concerns that disturb me?

The Word

The word of God comes down to us through the Scriptures. May the Holy Spirit enlighten my mind and my heart to respond to the gospel teachings. *(Please turn to the Scripture on the following pages. Inspiration points are there, should you need them. When you are ready, return here to continue.)*

Conversation

I begin to talk with Jesus about the Scripture I have just read. What part of it strikes a chord in me? Perhaps the words of a friend—or some story I have heard recently—will rise to the surface in my consciousness. If so, does the story throw light on what the Scripture passage may be saying to me?

Conclusion

Glory be to the Father, and to the Son, and to the Holy Spirit, as it was in the beginning, is now and ever shall be, world without end. Amen.

Sunday 24 March
Palm Sunday of the Passion of the Lord
Mark 14:1–15:47

It was two days before the Passover and the festival of Unleavened Bread. The chief priests and the scribes were looking for a way to arrest Jesus by stealth and kill him; for they said, 'Not during the festival, or there may be a riot among the people.'

While he was at Bethany in the house of Simon the leper, as he sat at the table, a woman came with an alabaster jar of very costly ointment of nard, and she broke open the jar and poured the ointment on his head. But some were there who said to one another in anger, 'Why was the ointment wasted in this way? For this ointment could have been sold for more than three hundred denarii, and the money given to the poor.' And they scolded her. But Jesus said, 'Let her alone; why do you trouble her? She has performed a good service for me. For you always have the poor with you, and you can show kindness to them whenever you wish; but you will not always have me. She has done what she could; she has anointed my body beforehand for its burial. Truly I tell you, wherever the good news is proclaimed in the whole world, what she has done will be told in remembrance of her.'

Then Judas Iscariot, who was one of the twelve, went to the chief priests in order to betray him to them. When they heard it, they were greatly pleased, and promised to give him money. So he began to look for an opportunity to betray him.

On the first day of Unleavened Bread, when the Passover lamb is sacrificed, his disciples said to him, 'Where do you want us to go and make the preparations for you to eat the Passover?' So he sent two of his disciples, saying to them, 'Go into the city, and a man carrying a jar of water will meet you; follow him, and wherever he enters, say to the owner of the house, "The Teacher asks, Where is my guest room where I may eat the Passover with my disciples?" He will show you a large room upstairs, furnished and ready. Make preparations for us there.' So the disciples set out and went to the city, and found everything as he had told them; and they prepared the Passover meal.

When it was evening, he came with the twelve. And when they had taken their places and were eating, Jesus said, 'Truly I tell you, one of you will betray me, one who is eating with me.' They began to be distressed and to say to him one after another, 'Surely, not I?' He said to them, 'It is one of the twelve, one who is dipping bread into the bowl with me. For the Son of Man goes as it is written of him, but woe to that one by whom the Son of Man is betrayed! It would have been better for that one not to have been born.'

While they were eating, he took a loaf of bread, and after blessing it he broke it, gave it to them, and said, 'Take; this is my body.' Then he took a cup, and after giving thanks he gave it to them, and all of them drank from it. He said to them, 'This is my blood of the covenant, which is poured out for many. Truly I tell you, I will never again drink of the fruit of the vine until that day when I drink it new in the kingdom of God.'

When they had sung the hymn, they went out to the Mount of Olives. And Jesus said to them, 'You will all become deserters; for it is written,

"I will strike the shepherd,
    and the sheep will be scattered."

But after I am raised up, I will go before you to Galilee.' Peter said to him, 'Even though all become deserters, I will not.' Jesus said to him, 'Truly I tell you, this day, this very night, before the cock crows twice, you will deny me three times.' But he said vehemently, 'Even though I must die with you, I will not deny you.' And all of them said the same.

They went to a place called Gethsemane; and he said to his disciples, 'Sit here while I pray.' He took with him Peter and James and John, and began to be distressed and agitated. And he said to them, 'I am deeply grieved, even to death; remain here, and keep awake.' And going a little farther, he threw himself on the ground and prayed that, if it were possible, the hour might pass from him. He said, 'Abba, Father, for you all things are possible; remove this cup from me; yet, not what I want, but what you want.' He came and found them sleeping; and he said to Peter, 'Simon, are you asleep? Could you not keep awake one hour? Keep awake and pray that you may not come into the time of trial; the spirit indeed is willing, but the flesh is weak.' And again he went away and prayed, saying the same words. And once more he came and found them sleeping, for their eyes were very heavy; and they did not know what to say to him. He came a third time and said to them, 'Are you still sleeping and taking your rest? Enough! The hour has come; the Son of Man is betrayed into the hands of sinners. Get up, let us be going. See, my betrayer is at hand.'

Immediately, while he was still speaking, Judas, one of the twelve, arrived; and with him there was a crowd with swords and clubs, from the chief priests, the scribes, and the elders. Now the betrayer had given them a sign, saying, 'The one I will kiss is the man; arrest him and lead him away under guard.' So when he came, he went up to him at once and said, 'Rabbi!' and kissed him. Then they laid hands on him and arrested him. But one of those who stood near drew his sword and struck the slave of the high priest, cutting off his ear. Then Jesus said to them,

'Have you come out with swords and clubs to arrest me as though I were a bandit? Day after day I was with you in the temple teaching, and you did not arrest me. But let the scriptures be fulfilled.' All of them deserted him and fled.

A certain young man was following him, wearing nothing but a linen cloth. They caught hold of him, but he left the linen cloth and ran off naked.

They took Jesus to the high priest; and all the chief priests, the elders, and the scribes were assembled. Peter had followed him at a distance, right into the courtyard of the high priest; and he was sitting with the guards, warming himself at the fire. Now the chief priests and the whole council were looking for testimony against Jesus to put him to death; but they found none. For many gave false testimony against him, and their testimony did not agree. Some stood up and gave false testimony against him, saying, 'We heard him say, "I will destroy this temple that is made with hands, and in three days I will build another, not made with hands."' But even on this point their testimony did not agree. Then the high priest stood up before them and asked Jesus, 'Have you no answer? What is it that they testify against you?' But he was silent and did not answer. Again the high priest asked him, 'Are you the Messiah, the Son of the Blessed One?' Jesus said, 'I am; and

"you will see the Son of Man
seated at the right hand of the Power",
and "coming with the clouds of heaven."'

Then the high priest tore his clothes and said, 'Why do we still need witnesses? You have heard his blasphemy! What is your decision?' All of them condemned him as deserving death. Some began to spit on him, to blindfold him, and to strike him, saying to him, 'Prophesy!' The guards also took him over and beat him.

While Peter was below in the courtyard, one of the servant-girls of the high priest came by. When she saw Peter warming himself, she stared at him and said, 'You also were with Jesus, the man from Nazareth.' But he denied it, saying, 'I do not know or understand what you are talking about.' And he went out into the forecourt. Then the cock crowed. And the servant-girl, on seeing him, began again to say to the bystanders, 'This man is one of them.' But again he denied it. Then after a little while the bystanders again said to Peter, 'Certainly you are one of them; for you are a Galilean.' But he began to curse, and he swore an oath, 'I do not know this man you are talking about.' At that moment the cock crowed for the second time. Then Peter remembered that Jesus had said to him, 'Before the cock crows twice, you will deny me three times.' And he broke down and wept.

As soon as it was morning, the chief priests held a consultation with the elders and scribes and the whole council. They bound Jesus, led him away, and handed him over to Pilate. Pilate asked him, 'Are you the King of the Jews?' He answered him, 'You say so.' Then the chief priests accused him of many things. Pilate asked him again, 'Have you no answer? See how many charges they bring against you.' But Jesus made no further reply, so that Pilate was amazed.

Now at the festival he used to release a prisoner for them, anyone for whom they asked. Now a man called Barabbas was in prison with the rebels who had committed murder during the insurrection. So the crowd came and began to ask Pilate to do for them according to his custom. Then he answered them, 'Do you want me to release for you the King of the Jews?' For he realized that it was out of jealousy that the chief priests had handed him over. But the chief priests stirred up the crowd to have him release Barabbas for them instead. Pilate spoke to them again, 'Then what do you wish me to do with the man you call the King of the Jews?' They shouted back, 'Crucify him!' Pilate asked them, 'Why, what evil has he done?' But they shouted all the more, 'Crucify him!' So Pilate, wishing to satisfy the crowd, released Barabbas for them; and after flogging Jesus, he handed him over to be crucified.

Then the soldiers led him into the courtyard of the palace (that is, the governor's headquarters); and they called together the whole cohort. And they clothed him in a purple cloak; and after twisting some thorns into a crown, they put it on him. And they began saluting him, 'Hail, King of the Jews!' They struck his head with a reed, spat upon him, and knelt down in homage to him. After mocking him, they stripped him of the purple cloak and put his own clothes on him. Then they led him out to crucify him.

They compelled a passer-by, who was coming in from the country, to carry his cross; it was Simon of Cyrene, the father of Alexander and Rufus. Then they brought Jesus to the place called Golgotha (which means the place of a skull). And they offered him wine mixed with myrrh; but he did not take it. And they crucified him, and divided his clothes among them, casting lots to decide what each should take.

It was nine o'clock in the morning when they crucified him. The inscription of the charge against him read, 'The King of the Jews.' And with him they crucified two bandits, one on his right and one on his left. Those who passed by derided him, shaking their heads and saying, 'Aha! You who would destroy the temple and build it in three days, save yourself, and come down from the cross!' In the same way the chief priests, along with the scribes, were also mocking him among themselves and saying, 'He saved others; he cannot save himself. Let the Messiah, the King of Israel, come down from the cross now, so that we may see and believe.' Those who were crucified with him also taunted him.

When it was noon, darkness came over the whole land until three in the afternoon. At three o'clock Jesus cried out with a loud voice, 'Eloi, Eloi, lama sabachthani?' which means, 'My God, my God, why have you forsaken me?' When some of the bystanders heard it, they said, 'Listen, he is calling for Elijah.' And someone ran, filled a sponge with sour wine, put it on a stick, and gave it to him to drink, saying, 'Wait, let us see whether Elijah will come to take him down.' Then Jesus gave a loud cry and breathed his last. And the curtain of the temple was torn in two, from top to bottom. Now when the centurion, who stood facing him, saw that in this way he breathed his last, he said, 'Truly this man was God's Son!'

There were also women looking on from a distance; among them were Mary Magdalene, and Mary the mother of James the younger and of Joses, and Salome. These used to follow him and provided for him when he was in Galilee; and there were many other women who had come up with him to Jerusalem.

When evening had come, and since it was the day of Preparation, that is, the day before the sabbath,

Joseph of Arimathea, a respected member of the council, who was also himself waiting expectantly for the kingdom of God, went boldly to Pilate and asked for the body of Jesus. Then Pilate wondered if he were already dead; and summoning the centurion, he asked him whether he had been dead for some time. When he learned from the centurion that he was dead, he granted the body to Joseph. Then Joseph bought a linen cloth, and taking down the body, wrapped it in the linen cloth, and laid it in a tomb that had been hewn out of the rock. He then rolled a stone against the door of the tomb. Mary Magdalene and Mary the mother of Joses saw where the body was laid.

- Jesus could be described as the suffering servant in Mark's Gospel. There is the challenge of staying with him to understand suffering as we tend to struggle to find meaning in it. We pray to be strengthened by the Passion, remembering that it is Jesus we want, not suffering.

- The welcome of Jesus to Jerusalem was in marked contrast to the events of the following days. Spending time with key people in the drama helps us to enter more fully into the passion of Jesus and of the world. We pray that we may be able to stay with you, Lord, amid the trials you endured.

Monday 25 March

John 12:1–11

Six days before the Passover Jesus came to Bethany, the home of Lazarus, whom he had raised from the dead. There they gave a dinner for him. Martha served, and Lazarus was one of those at the table with him. Mary took a pound of costly perfume made of pure nard, anointed Jesus' feet, and wiped them with her hair. The house was filled with the fragrance of the perfume. But Judas Iscariot, one of his disciples (the one who was about to betray him), said, 'Why was this perfume not sold for three hundred denarii and the money given to the poor?' (He said this not because he cared about the poor, but because he was a thief; he kept the common purse and used to steal what was put into it.) Jesus said, 'Leave her alone. She bought it so that she might keep it for the day of my burial. You always have the poor with you, but you do not always have me.'

When the great crowd of the Jews learned that he was there, they came not only because of Jesus but also to see Lazarus, whom he had raised from the dead. So the chief priests planned to put Lazarus to death as well, since it was on account of him that many of the Jews were deserting and were believing in Jesus.

• The context was a dinner in the home of Lazarus with the apostles shortly before Passover. Jesus accepted the welcome. Meanwhile, the chief priests were planning to kill him and Lazarus. May we gather with you as your friends and be willing to live as your anointed ones.

- Mary's generosity in pouring out costly perfume contrasted with the miserly attitude of Judas. She portrayed the self-giving of Jesus. Lord, give us generous hearts that can give without counting the cost, that seek to serve you in the poor of our time.

Tuesday 26 March
John 13:21–33, 36–38

After saying this Jesus was troubled in spirit, and declared, 'Very truly, I tell you, one of you will betray me.' The disciples looked at one another, uncertain of whom he was speaking. One of his disciples—the one whom Jesus loved—was reclining next to him; Simon Peter therefore motioned to him to ask Jesus of whom he was speaking. So while reclining next to Jesus, he asked him, 'Lord, who is it?' Jesus answered, 'It is the one to whom I give this piece of bread when I have dipped it in the dish.' So when he had dipped the piece of bread, he gave it to Judas son of Simon Iscariot. After he received the piece of bread, Satan entered into him. Jesus said to him, 'Do quickly what you are going to do.' Now no one at the table knew why he said this to him. Some thought that, because Judas had the common purse, Jesus was telling him, 'Buy what we need for the festival'; or, that he should give something to the poor. So, after receiving the piece of bread, he immediately went out. And it was night.

When he had gone out, Jesus said, 'Now the Son of Man has been glorified, and God has been glorified in him. If God has been glorified in him, God will also glorify him in himself and will glorify him at once. Little children, I am with you only a little longer. You will look for me; and as I said to the Jews so now I say to you, "Where I am going, you cannot come."

Simon Peter said to him, 'Lord, where are you going?' Jesus answered, 'Where I am going, you cannot follow me now; but you will follow afterwards.' Peter said to him, 'Lord, why can I not follow you now? I will lay down my life for you.' Jesus answered, 'Will you lay down your life for me? Very truly, I tell you, before the cock crows, you will have denied me three times.'

- Jesus told the disciples that one of them would betray him. Peter's curiosity was aroused and he sought the answer through the beloved disciple. This was supposed to be a table of union, with a bond between those who shared it. Lord, make us aware of the times we have betrayed loyalty and not been faithful to your covenant with us.

- Judas, having taken the bread, went out. It was night. That symbolised the internal darkness that had taken over. Lord, help us to recognise when darkness prevails in our lives, when we become negative and pessimistic, so that we may turn back to you, the true light.

Wednesday 27 March
Matthew 26:14–25

Then one of the twelve, who was called Judas Iscariot, went to the chief priests and said, 'What will you give me if I betray him to you?' They paid him thirty pieces of silver. And from that moment he began to look for an opportunity to betray him.

On the first day of Unleavened Bread the disciples came to Jesus, saying, 'Where do you want us to make the preparations for you to eat the Passover?' He said, 'Go into the city to a certain man, and say to him, "The Teacher says, My time is near; I will keep the Passover at your house with my disciples."' So the disciples did as Jesus had directed them, and they prepared the Passover meal.

When it was evening, he took his place with the twelve; and while they were eating, he said, 'Truly I tell you, one of you will betray me.' And they became greatly distressed and began to say to him one after another, 'Surely not I, Lord?' He answered, 'The one who has dipped his hand into the bowl with me will betray me. The Son of Man goes as it is written of him, but woe to that one by whom the Son of Man is betrayed! It would have been better for that one not to have been born.' Judas, who betrayed him, said, 'Surely not I, Rabbi?' He replied, 'You have said so.'

- Joseph was sold by his own brothers for twenty pieces of silver and ended up being their saviour (Genesis 37:25–28). Judas, who was not known for his honesty (John 12:6), betrayed Jesus for thirty pieces of silver. May we acknowledge our greed and self-interest so that we are more free to serve you in your people.

- Jesus indicated that his time was near and asked the disciples to prepare the Passover meal. He knew that Judas would betray him. Lord, may we be honest in bringing our struggles to you as we recognise our capacity to deny and betray you.

Thursday 28 March
Holy Thursday
John 13:1–15

Now before the festival of the Passover, Jesus knew that his hour had come to depart from this world and go to the Father. Having loved his own who were in the world, he loved them to the end. The devil had already put it into the heart of Judas son of Simon Iscariot to betray him. And during supper Jesus, knowing that the Father had given all things into his hands, and that he had come from God and was going to God, got up from the table, took off his outer robe, and tied a towel around himself. Then he poured water into a basin and began to wash the disciples' feet and to wipe them with the towel that was tied around him. He came to Simon Peter, who said to him, 'Lord, are you going to wash my feet?' Jesus answered, 'You do not know now what I am doing, but later you will understand.' Peter said to him, 'You will never wash my feet.' Jesus answered, 'Unless I wash you, you have no share with me.' Simon Peter said to him, 'Lord, not my feet only but also my hands and my head!' Jesus said to him, 'One who has bathed does not need to wash, except for the feet, but is entirely clean. And you are clean, though not all of you.' For he knew who was to betray him; for this reason he said, 'Not all of you are clean.'

After he had washed their feet, had put on his robe, and had returned to the table, he said to them, 'Do you know what I have done to you? You call me Teacher and Lord—and you are right, for that is what I am. So if I, your Lord and Teacher, have washed your feet, you also ought to wash one another's feet. For I have set you an example, that you also should do as I have done to you.'

- Jesus knew that his hour had come to depart this world. Having loved his own, he loved them to the end. Jesus had clarity on what was happening, but the disciples were confused. We pray for the freedom to listen to Jesus and to be less concerned about our own interests.

- It was servants who washed the master's feet (Luke 12:35–40). Jesus reversed the process. He set an example for us. Lord, like Peter, we tend to protest at you serving us. Give us a greater faith and love so that we can see you in others and imitate you in love.

Friday 29 March
Good Friday
John 18:1–19:42

After Jesus had spoken these words, he went out with his disciples across the Kidron valley to a place where there was a garden, which he and his disciples entered. Now Judas, who betrayed him, also knew the place, because Jesus often met there with his disciples. So Judas brought a detachment of soldiers together with police from the chief priests and the Pharisees, and they came there with lanterns and torches and weapons. Then Jesus, knowing all that was to happen to him, came forward and asked them, 'For whom are you looking?' They answered, 'Jesus of Nazareth.'

Jesus replied, 'I am he.' Judas, who betrayed him, was standing with them. When Jesus said to them, 'I am he', they stepped back and fell to the ground. Again he asked them, 'For whom are you looking?' And they said, 'Jesus of Nazareth.' Jesus answered, 'I told you that I am he. So if you are looking for me, let these men go.' This was to fulfil the word that he had spoken, 'I did not lose a single one of those whom you gave me.' Then Simon Peter, who had a sword, drew it, struck the high priest's slave, and cut off his right ear. The slave's name was Malchus. Jesus said to Peter, 'Put your sword back into its sheath. Am I not to drink the cup that the Father has given me?'

So the soldiers, their officer, and the Jewish police arrested Jesus and bound him. First they took him to Annas, who was the father-in-law of Caiaphas, the high priest that year. Caiaphas was the one who had advised the Jews that it was better to have one person die for the people.

Simon Peter and another disciple followed Jesus. Since that disciple was known to the high priest, he went with Jesus into the courtyard of the high priest, but Peter was standing outside at the gate. So the other disciple, who was known to the high priest, went out, spoke to the woman who guarded the gate, and brought Peter in. The woman said to Peter, 'You are not also one of this man's disciples, are you?' He said, 'I am not.' Now the slaves and the police had made a charcoal fire because it was cold, and they were standing round it and warming themselves. Peter also was standing with them and warming himself.

Then the high priest questioned Jesus about his disciples and about his teaching. Jesus answered, 'I have spoken openly to the world; I have always taught in synagogues and in the temple, where all the Jews come together. I have said nothing in secret. Why do you ask me? Ask those who heard what I said to them; they know what I said.' When he had said this, one of the police standing nearby struck Jesus on the face, saying, 'Is that how you answer the high priest?' Jesus answered, 'If I have spoken wrongly, testify to the wrong. But if I have spoken rightly, why do you strike me?' Then Annas sent him bound to Caiaphas the high priest.

Now Simon Peter was standing and warming himself. They asked him, 'You are not also one of his disciples, are you?' He denied it and said, 'I am not.' One of the slaves of the high priest, a relative of the man whose ear Peter had cut off, asked, 'Did I not see you in the garden with him?' Again Peter denied it, and at that moment the cock crowed.

Then they took Jesus from Caiaphas to Pilate's headquarters. It was early in the morning. They themselves did not enter the headquarters, so as to avoid ritual defilement and to be able to eat the Passover. So Pilate went out to them and said, 'What accusation do you bring against this man?' They answered, 'If this man were not a criminal, we would not have handed him over to you.' Pilate said to them, 'Take him yourselves and judge him according to your law.' The Jews replied, 'We are not permitted to put anyone to death.' (This was to fulfil what Jesus had said when he indicated the kind of death he was to die.)

Then Pilate entered the headquarters again, summoned Jesus, and asked him, 'Are you the King of the Jews?' Jesus answered, 'Do you ask this on your own, or did others tell you about me?' Pilate replied, 'I am not a Jew, am I? Your own nation and the chief priests have handed you over to me. What have you done?' Jesus answered, 'My kingdom is not from this world. If my kingdom were from this world, my followers would be fighting to keep me from being handed over to the Jews. But as it is, my kingdom is not from here.' Pilate asked him, 'So you are a king?' Jesus answered, 'You say that I am a king. For this I was born, and for this I came into the world, to testify to the truth. Everyone who belongs to the truth listens to my voice.' Pilate asked him, 'What is truth?'

After he had said this, he went out to the Jews again and told them, 'I find no case against him. But you have a custom that I release someone for you at the Passover. Do you want me to release for you the King of the Jews?' They shouted in reply, 'Not this man, but Barabbas!' Now Barabbas was a bandit.

Then Pilate took Jesus and had him flogged. And the soldiers wove a crown of thorns and put it on his head, and they dressed him in a purple robe. They kept coming up to him, saying, 'Hail, King of the Jews!' and striking him on the face. Pilate went out again and said to them, 'Look, I am bringing him out to you to let you know that I find no case against him.' So Jesus came out, wearing the crown of thorns and the purple robe. Pilate said to them, 'Here is the man!' When the chief priests and the police saw him, they shouted, 'Crucify him! Crucify him!' Pilate said to them, 'Take him yourselves and crucify him; I find no case against him.' The Jews answered him, 'We have a law, and according to that law he ought to die because he has claimed to be the Son of God.'

Now when Pilate heard this, he was more afraid than ever. He entered his headquarters again and asked Jesus, 'Where are you from?' But Jesus gave him no answer. Pilate therefore said to him, 'Do you refuse to speak to me? Do you not know that I have power to release you, and power to crucify you?' Jesus answered him, 'You would have no power over me unless it had been given you from above; therefore the one who handed me over to you is guilty of a greater sin.' From then on Pilate tried to release him, but the Jews cried out, 'If you release this man, you are no friend of the emperor. Everyone who claims to be a king sets himself against the emperor.'

When Pilate heard these words, he brought Jesus outside and sat on the judge's bench at a place called The Stone Pavement, or in Hebrew Gabbatha. Now it was the day of Preparation for the Passover; and it was about noon. He said to the Jews, 'Here is your King!' They cried out, 'Away with him! Away with him! Crucify him!' Pilate asked them, 'Shall I crucify your King?' The chief priests answered, 'We have no king but the emperor.' Then he handed him over to them to be crucified.

So they took Jesus; and carrying the cross by himself, he went out to what is called The Place of the Skull, which in Hebrew is called Golgotha. There they crucified him, and with him two others, one on either side, with Jesus between them. Pilate also had an inscription written and put on the cross. It read, 'Jesus of Nazareth, the King of the Jews.' Many of the Jews read this inscription, because the place where Jesus was crucified was near the city; and it was written in Hebrew, in Latin, and in Greek. Then the chief priests of the Jews said to Pilate, 'Do not write, "The King of the Jews", but, "This man said, I am King of the Jews."' Pilate answered, 'What I have written I have written.' When the soldiers had crucified Jesus, they took his clothes and divided them into four parts, one for each soldier. They also took his tunic; now the tunic was seamless, woven in one piece from the top. So they said to one another, 'Let us not tear it, but cast lots for it to see who will get it.' This was to fulfil what the scripture says,

> 'They divided my clothes among themselves,
> and for my clothing they cast lots.'

And that is what the soldiers did.

Meanwhile, standing near the cross of Jesus were his mother, and his mother's sister, Mary the wife of Clopas, and Mary Magdalene. When Jesus saw his mother and the disciple whom he loved standing beside her, he said to his mother, 'Woman, here is your son.' Then he said to the disciple, 'Here is your mother.' And from that hour the disciple took her into his own home.

After this, when Jesus knew that all was now finished, he said (in order to fulfil the scripture), 'I am thirsty.' A jar full of sour wine was standing there. So they put a sponge full of the wine on a branch of hyssop and held it to his mouth. When Jesus had received the wine, he said, 'It is finished.' Then he bowed his head and gave up his spirit.

Since it was the day of Preparation, the Jews did not want the bodies left on the cross during the sabbath, especially because that sabbath was a day of great solemnity. So they asked Pilate to have the legs of the crucified men broken and the bodies removed. Then the soldiers came and broke the legs of the first and of the other who had been crucified with him.

But when they came to Jesus and saw that he was already dead, they did not break his legs. Instead, one of the soldiers pierced his side with a spear, and at once blood and water came out. (He who saw this has testified so that you also may believe. His testimony is true, and he knows that he tells the truth.) These things occurred so that the scripture might be fulfilled, 'None of his bones shall be broken.' And again another passage of scripture says, 'They will look on the one whom they have pierced.'

After these things, Joseph of Arimathea, who was a disciple of Jesus, though a secret one because of his fear of the Jews, asked Pilate to let him take away the body of Jesus. Pilate gave him permission; so he came and removed his body. Nicodemus, who had at first come to Jesus by night, also came, bringing a mixture of myrrh and aloes, weighing about a hundred pounds. They took the body of Jesus and wrapped it with the spices in linen cloths, according to the burial custom of the Jews. Now there was a garden in the place where he was crucified, and in the garden there was a new tomb in which no one had ever been laid. And so, because it was the Jewish day of Preparation, and the tomb was nearby, they laid Jesus there.

- The Passion is a love story of total self-giving. Through his prayer in the garden, Jesus came to peace in facing what lay ahead. He acknowledged who he was to those who came to arrest him—'I am he.' Lord, help us in our search and our struggles to find you so that we may have the strength and peace to walk onwards with you.

• It could appear as if it were Pilate who was on trial. His position as governor and the threat of the crowd was enough to have him go against his own beliefs and hand Jesus over. We pray that we may hand over our lives to Jesus and have the courage to stand by the innocent who are falsely accused at this time.

Saturday 30 March
Holy Saturday
Mark 16:1–7

When the sabbath was over, Mary Magdalene, and Mary the mother of James, and Salome bought spices, so that they might go and anoint him. And very early on the first day of the week, when the sun had risen, they went to the tomb. They had been saying to one another, 'Who will roll away the stone for us from the entrance to the tomb?' When they looked up, they saw that the stone, which was very large, had already been rolled back. As they entered the tomb, they saw a young man, dressed in a white robe, sitting on the right side; and they were alarmed. But he said to them, 'Do not be alarmed; you are looking for

Jesus of Nazareth, who was crucified. He has been raised; he is not here. Look, there is the place they laid him. But go, tell his disciples and Peter that he is going ahead of you to Galilee; there you will see him, just as he told you.'

- It is the day after the funeral, with time to remember, to share stories, to take quiet time. Perhaps Peter and Judas, as flawed disciples, may speak to us in our feeble attempts to be loyal. Lord, help us to appreciate more fully who you are and what you have done for us.

- What was the day like for Mary? The prophecy of the sword of sorrow piercing her heart had become more real (Luke 2:34–35). It was painful for her to see her beloved son of compassion and love being treated so cruelly. May we draw strength from the fidelity of Mary in staying with Jesus to the end.

Sunday 31 March
Easter Sunday of the Resurrection of the Lord
John 20:1–9

Early on the first day of the week, while it was still dark, Mary Magdalene came to the tomb and saw that the stone had been removed from the tomb. So she ran and went to Simon Peter and the other disciple, the one whom Jesus loved, and said to them, 'They have taken the Lord out of the tomb, and we do not know where they have laid him.' Then Peter and the other disciple set out and went towards the tomb. The two were running together, but the other disciple outran Peter and reached the tomb first. He bent down to look in and saw the linen wrappings lying there, but he did not go in. Then Simon Peter came, following him, and went into the tomb. He saw the linen wrappings lying there, and the cloth that had been on Jesus' head, not lying with the linen wrappings but rolled up in a place by itself. Then the other disciple, who reached the tomb first, also went in, and he saw and believed; for as yet they did not understand the scripture, that he must rise from the dead.

- There was urgency to the action of Mary Magdalene. It was like the dawn of a new creation, with light scattering darkness. Finding the stone rolled back, she ran for help. Lord, help us, as there are times when we feel that you have been removed from our lives and we do not know where to find you.

- The two disciples ran to the tomb to find it empty, with the linen wrappings lying there. Its meaning was not clear. Then the intuitive beloved disciple 'saw and believed'. We pray that we may acknowledge the empty tombs in our lives and our slowness to interpret the many signs given to us.

Suscipe

Take, Lord, and receive all my liberty,
my memory, my understanding,
and my entire will,

all I have and call my own.
You have given all to me.

To you, Lord, I return it.
Everything is yours; do with it what you will.
Give me only your love and your grace;
that is enough for me.

—St. Ignatius of Loyola

Prayer to Know God's Will

May it please the supreme and divine Goodness
To give us all abundant grace
Ever to know his most holy will
And perfectly to fulfill it.

—St. Ignatius of Loyola